DEAR

ME

L♥VE

YOUR

SELF

THE POETRY SHOP

DEAR ME LOVE YOURSELF

BY MOON CHILD

To those of you
Who have fallen
On these pages
This is *meant to be*
It's destiny
Make this world
And these words
Yours

dear me

*"Your visions will become
clear only when you can
look into your own heart.
Who looks outside,
dreams; who looks inside,
awakes."*

Carl Gustav Jung

The spring seems so far away
In this harsh winter
Can my dreams bloom?
Like the glory of the snow
Will it make it through the cold snow?

What is the meaning of life, and what purpose do I carry in its endless flow?

It's okay
Not to be okay
On some days
The sun may shine less
But it will still set
In the most beautiful way

Do I see the beauty in the world, and how might I uncover more of it?

Countless rides
On Ferris wheels
Countless trips
To the moon
Countless trips
To the stars
Between earth and sky
Back and forth
For my hopes to climb
For my heart to rehab

What values do I hold sacred, guiding me as the stars guide the night?

A bit lost
A bit scared
Thinking about the past
Wondering about the future
And my dreams stuck in between

Do I find myself more in the company of others, or within the solitude of my own thoughts?

Lost in the desert
I swallow every pearl of sand
Hoping I can find the sea
But I ended up being drown

To whom do I place my faith, and why does their light shine brightest?

Lost between
The ifs, buts or maybes
And all these question marks
Reviving my regrets
And remorse
Over and over again

In the mirror of my soul, do I see the reflection of the world's beauty, or do I seek it in places yet unknown?

Lost
Between the sea and the sky
And my stuck wishes in between

What language of love do I speak, and how do others speak it to me?

Looking for the fragments of my dreams
What were the things
I dreamed about?
What was I craving for?
Who stole them from me?
Was it me?

Do I compare my path to others', or do I walk with faith in my own footsteps?

book: *dear me, love yourself*

Endlessly looking for answers
I found myself asking more questions
What was I made for?

When the world feels heavy, what small moments lift my soul?

No longer what I were
Not what I wanted to be
But I am still *me*
Right?

What is it that I hold dear within myself?

If I am not
What I wanted to be
If I don't want to be
That person anymore
What's wrong with living like that?

How can I protect these precious things?

A never ending loop
Figuring out my life
Always wandering
In search of something

What are the things hidden deep inside me?

Adulting
Feels like
Walking down the stairs in darkness
And tripping from time to time

**Am I content with who
I have become, or are there
pieces yet to be molded?**

Different stages of life
So many feelings
And dreams
So many hopes
And despair
Choices and regrets
Stuck between each stage

What simple joys bring my heart to life, regardless of the season?

Not everything can be fixed
I tried hard to do it
Sometimes too hard
That I would be the one
That need to be fixed

What deep passions ignite my spirit, urging me forward on the road of discovery?

I can't control everything in life
Sometimes
I just have to let it go

What is the greatest strength I possess, and how does it carry me through the storm?

Life is moving fast
Too fast
Don't wanna miss my time
Wanna make it mine

What weaknesses do I face, and how might I grow from them, like a tree bending toward the sun?

Time flies so fast
Wanna press the repeat button
No ifs, buts or maybes
But why make life as a tape recorder
When it can be a rollercoaster?

What does my inner voice say when I listen closely, and what wisdom does it offer me?

Sometimes
I just wanna press the pause button
Slow down a little bit

How do I celebrate my victories, or do I let them slip by unnoticed?

I wish
I could press the rewind button
Fix all the moments that got messed up

What compliment would fill my heart with the purest joy, if I were to hear it whispered on the wind?

Don't drown yourself with questions
You don't have answers to
Life will give you the answer
When it's the right time

When I was young, what dreams did I weave for my future, and how do they compare to the life I live now?

A loud voice in my head
The silence makes it louder

Am I living the life I once imagined, or have the winds of time led me to unexpected shores?

Begging my mind for some silence
So many thoughts
Too many worries
Wanna dim the lights
Inside my mind
Wanna tam the voices
Trapped inside

What advice would I offer the me from five or ten years ago, knowing what I know now?

Wanna clear my mind
Wanna shut all those thoughts
Wanna get rid of my shadows
Open my heart wide
And leave a smile on my face

What moments in my life am I most proud of, and how do they shape the person I am today?

Wanna quiet my mind
No more worries
In the dark night
No more fears
In the heavy silence

What accomplishment stands as the highest peak in my journey, casting its shadow over all that came before?

I want to be one with this shadow
This endless labyrinth
This part of me
My unconscious

What has been my greatest failure, and what lesson has it whispered to me in the quiet of reflection?

The frog will disperse
Taking away your despair
Don't worry too much

If today were my last, what would I regret not having done, and how can I move toward it now?

There were times
I felt that I wasn't good enough
Times
I felt that I didn't belong

What is missing from my life, and how can I reach out and claim it?

Not good enough for this
Not good enough for that
What about this?
What about that?
Enough is enough

What is the best piece of advice I have received, and how has it shaped the choices I make?

One word
Enough to taint
All my confidence
Forgot all the kind words
And focused on the trivial ones

What is the most sacred place in my heart, where I feel safe, whole, and at peace?

Wanna give myself
Just half of the love
I give to others

What is the one thing I wish to learn more of, as if the universe beckons me closer with its endless mysteries?

Sometimes
I just wanna lean on myself
Take a little rest

What does my heart tell me when I listen to my dreams at night?

love yourself

*"And God said love your
enemy and I obeyed him
and loved myself."*

Khalil GIBRAN

Don't wanna burst in tears
I wanna burst into
A beautiful butterfly

What would make my life richer, deeper, and more meaningful than it is today?

There is magic in you
In every tear
In every smile
Your tears shine
And your smile
Reflects the light
You are simply
Magical

What song lifts my spirit when the weight of the world feels too heavy, a melody that always brings me back to joy?

Like the pink cherry blossoms
I wanna bloom again
Even if my petals fall
I wanna fall in the most beautiful way
Just like the pink cherry blossoms

Where would I go, if given wings to live anywhere in the world, and what would I seek there?

Wanna fall and rise at once
Be my sunset and sunrise
Wanna fall and rise
In the most beautiful way

What advice would I offer my younger self, the child who once dreamed so freely?

Your happiness is between your hands
Take a step forward
It looks too far
But it's so close

What is the one thing I will never do, or never have the chance to do, and what makes it unattainable?

Not all your dreams
Will become reality
But all what you believe in
All what you are manifesting
With your heart wide open
Will happen

What does love mean to me, and how do I express it in the world around me?

Good things happen for a reason
Bad things happen for a reason too

What is the one thing I look for in those I love, in a friend, a companion, or a partner?

My soul
You are inside me
But sometimes, I feel
You are so far from me
Wanna feel your warm
Want you to keep me warm

How do I show those I care for that they are cherished, and how do I wish to be shown love in return?

Hidden deep inside my soul
I wanna pull it out
I wanna discover the real me
And embrace it
In an endless symphony

Who is the one person whose presence fills my life with gratitude, and what am I thankful for in them?

Until spring comes again
And flowers bloom
Until birds start breeding
And butterflies come out
Until the pink cherry blossom falls
I will wait for you

What is the nicest thing
I have ever done for another,
and how did it change me?

Like the rain
On autumn's nights
Knocking at the window
I wanna knock at your door
I wanna be your lullaby
In those dark nights

**What is the greatest gift
I have received from
someone, and how did it
touch my soul?**

Wanna be brave enough
To find you
And tell you
How much I miss you
How much I love you
My inner child

**What makes me laugh until
I forget myself, that pure joy
that bubbles up from within?**

Millions of stars in the sky
Wanna borrow one
Wanna put in my heart
Wanna give it to my inner self
For myself to shine

What is the compliment I long to hear, that I feel touches my heart at its deepest core?

Wanna give you
All the stars in the sky
Wanna make you shine
Wanna hold you tight

What do I search for in a relationship, and how do I offer myself in return?

Wanna be my sun
In the cloudy sky
Wanna be my star
In the darkest sky
Wanna find my spark
Hidden somewhere inside me

How do I define my inner self, the part that no one else sees but I know so well?

Wanna be an astronaut
Wanna travel throughout the universe
Wanna touch the stars
Wanna see your shiniest spark

What are the fears that hold me, and how might I rise above them with courage and grace?

There is endless magic
Inside you
Shiny skies
And starry nights
Just open your eyes

What is the greatest lesson life has taught me so far, and how has it shaped the person I am becoming?

If there is a sun
I wanna day dream
If there is a moon
I wanna night dream
If there is a star
I want it to heal my scar

Do I allow myself to celebrate the milestones I have crossed, or do I let them fade into the distance without a second thought?

Wanna become
My comfort and shield
To take away
My sadness and pain

**Am I content with who
I have become, or is there
more that I wish to unfold
within me?**

Wanna be my light
In the pitch dark nights
Shining me
Precious me

How might I awaken to the whispers of my soul, and see myself as I truly am?

book: *dear me, love yourself*

Wanna make a little room in my heart
Wanna make it my safe place
Where I can sweep my tears
And rebuild my hopes and dreams

In what ways can I paint my days with the brushstrokes of creativity, and breathe life into my dreams?

Wanna be my best friend
My soulmate
Wanna be my light in the dark
And my rehab

**How can I wrap my heart
in the warmth of self-love,
nurturing it like a garden
in bloom?**

Dear me
I wanna keep you close
Wanna have you in every thought
In every decision and step

**What part of me calls for
healing, a piece of my being
waiting to unfold?**

Promise
When the sky gets dark
Don't throw yourself away
Be your most beautiful lullaby

**Is the chase for perfection
slowly eroding the truth of who
I am beneath the surface?**

You are the one
Who can make you feel alright
In the blink of an eye

**Does the weight of wanting it
all make my heart feel small,
like I'm never enough?**

I wanna be my music
The most beautiful one
An endless lullaby
The one that will always console me

What is the invisible barrier that keeps my dreams distant, and how might I rise beyond it?

Turn your radio
The one in your heart
It's worth listening to

What can I do today to make the path brighter, more radiant than it was yesterday?

Hold yourself tightly
Listen to yourself carefully
Embrace yourself fully

What pursuit stirs my heart, worthy of chasing even if it slips through my fingers?

You fall in love
With the little things
Why won't you fall in love with yourself?
Just fall in love
With all the beautiful things

How often do I pause to honor my own journey, and celebrate the quiet victories I've won?

I want my eyes to shine
When I talk about myself
As they shine
When I talk about the things
I love the most

What stirs the storm inside me—anger, sorrow, anxiety, or the weight of unspoken stress?

Accept that people can not all love you
But never accept
That you don't love yourself
Never

Do the thoughts that dance through my mind sing of love, or hum with the echoes of doubt?

You give me time
You give me love
And attention
I wanna do the same with me

In what moments do I wear the mask of happiness, while my heart silently yearns for more?

Wanna be a cheerleader
Wanna call my name high
Cheering for myself
All the way long

How do I quietly undermine my own joy, trapping myself in a web of self-sabotage?

Wanna love you
Just the way you are
Wanna love me
Just the way I am
Wanna hold you tight
Wanna hold me tight

**What old stories do I carry
with me, tattered pages of the
past I can't seem to release?**

Wanna be loved
With my flaws and imperfections
Wanna be loved
Unconditionally

What soft lies do I tell myself, and why do I weave them like threads in a tapestry of illusion?

I will find beauty
In every piece of myself
I will feel it in my heart
And see it with my own eyes

What spark of excitement flickers within me, calling me to embrace the unknown?

There is beauty in everything
There is even more beauty
In the smallest things
There is beauty inside you
Just keep your heart wide open
To fully embrace yourself

What longings live deep inside me, dreams unspoken but not forgotten?

Hidden in the back of my eyes
I will put it in my heart
To finally see it by my own eyes
This beautiful me

**What joy have I left behind,
a simple pleasure I've not
touched in too long?**

Wanna be full of colors
Wanna be blue
Wanna be red
Wanna be orange
Wanna be yellow
Wanna be green
Wanna be indigo
Wanna be violet
Wanna be an eternal rainbow

What must I release from my heart, so it can be light enough to dance in the sun?

Wanna put
A little blue in my sky
Don't wanna be blue
Just wanna be a sunshine

What is the burden I carry that no longer serves me, and how can I lay it down?

The blooming flowers
The rising sun
The shiny blue sky
I can finally see it
I can finally feel it
The beauty around me

What does my soul crave to feel whole, to awaken to the fullness of joy?

I wanna be my spring
I wanna be my summer
My umbrella on a rainy day
My blanket on a cold night
Wanna be my spring
And my summer
All together

What makes my spirit come alive, like the sun breaking through a cloudy sky?

Like the spring is fated to come
You will have your spring
Cause it's your fate
Your destiny

Do I feel free, or are there unseen chains that bind my heart and mind?

Wanna be like the sun
Slowly sinking in the ocean
And be reborn in another
Wanna be my sunrise
And my sunset
All together

Am I truly myself, or have I become a reflection of someone else's expectations?

My most beautiful sunrise
My most beautiful sunset
And my shiniest days
Are all ahead

Do I feel at peace in my skin, or does it whisper of discomfort I dare not face?

Like birds
Flying over the ocean
Wanna be
Wild
And
Free

What does my body speak
to me in the quiet moments,
when I pause to listen?

I've been looking for answers
Through the clouds of dawn
In the morning dew
As the sun rises
And the sky gets blue
When the sun faints
And the dusky twilight
Leaves the space to the starry night
I found no answers
But endless reasons
To enjoy the magic of me

If I could paint a picture of the perfect day, what colors would fill the canvas of my life?

I wanna be the morning dew
I wanna be the sun's first shines
Full of hope and joy
Ready to rise
Ready to reflect the light

What does a "perfect day" mean to me, when the world aligns with my heart's desires?

The smell of grass covered in dew
The singing birds
The blooming flowers
The rising sun
The shiny blue sky
I can finally see it
I can finally feel it
The beauty
Inside this reborning world

Who in my life pulls me into darkness, draining the light I've worked so hard to nurture?

If I can be reborn one day
I wanna be reborn in your arms
Wanna listen to your heartbeat
Wanna make it my heart's melody

**What relationships in my
life feel heavy, like a weight
I can no longer carry?**

If I can be reborn again
I will still choose you
Six times
A million times
A billion times
Endless times
I will still choose me

What have I been avoiding, and why does it feel so difficult to face?

I will love me
Until the day I die
I'm all yours
Beautiful me
Precious soul of mine

Which bonds wrap around me like sunlight, nourishing me with their warmth and care?

For once
I wanna keep my eyes on the skyline
I will make it my baseline
Wanna cherish every moment
Spent together on earth

**What boundaries must
I create to protect my
peace, to keep the toxic out
and let the good in?**

I wanna find strength
Looking at the sun
Be born and reborn
Again and again

What excess do I long to shed, to clear space for the things that truly matter?

Wanna believe in magic
The magic of self-love

Where in my heart do I need to forgive myself, and set the past free?

Be hungry for love
Be hungry for self-love
You come first

**When did I last welcome a
new soul into my circle,
and what did that
connection bring to my life?**

Wanna give you love
Wanna give you
All the gold in the world
Wanna make your sun rise sooner
Wanna make you shine
Just wanna hold you tight

If I could speak to the me from five years ago, what words of wisdom would I offer?

Drown yourself in love
Down yourself in compassion
Don't deprive yourself from forgiveness
You are the most important

In what ways do I hold myself back, afraid of the heights I could reach?

Embrace yourself
With love
Hold you
In your heart

What unseen force keeps me from stepping boldly toward my dreams, and how can I break free?

Let yourself be bathed with
Kindness
Compassion
And
LOVE

What goal stirs within me, a quiet longing that I dare not speak aloud?

Imagine
Loving yourself
Like no other

What adventure have I left behind, a path untaken that still calls me with gentle persistence?

Nothing is eternal
But the love for yourself is

Do I sometimes dream of running from it all, seeking solace in an unknown place?

Love yourself
With devotion
You deserve
A standing ovation

What boundary must I set in my life to protect my peace and well-being?

201

book: *dear me, love yourself*

Wanna write in capital letters
Wanna turn up the speakers
LOVE YOURSELF

What moments in my life deserve to be celebrated, no matter how small or fleeting?

I am worthy
I am loved
I love myself

What blessings in my daily life fill my heart with gratitude, like raindrops on dry earth?

Dear me, I promise
To hold you from this day forward
For better for worse
For richer for poorer
In sickness and in health
To love and to cherish
Till death us do part

What future possibilities fill me with excitement, waiting to unfold like the petals of a flower?

Dear me
You are
My most beautiful poem

What beautiful promises will you make to yourself?

Your Mind's Symphony

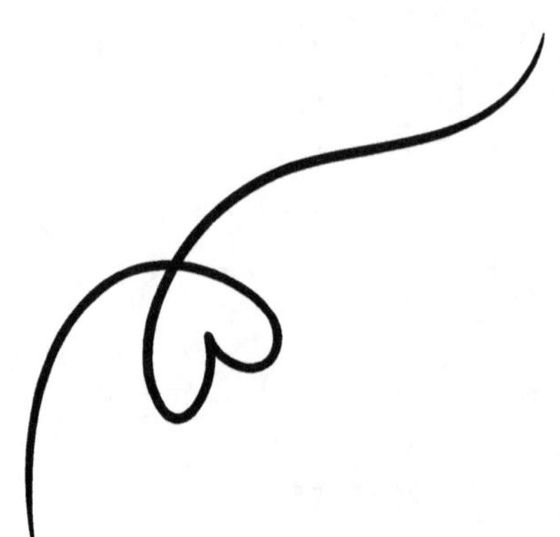

Your Heart's Symphony

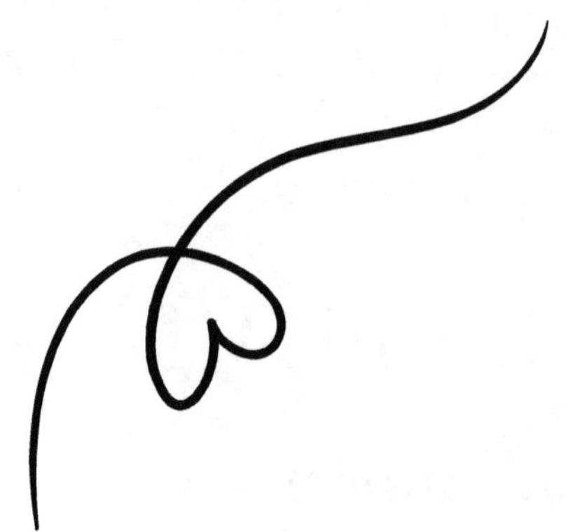

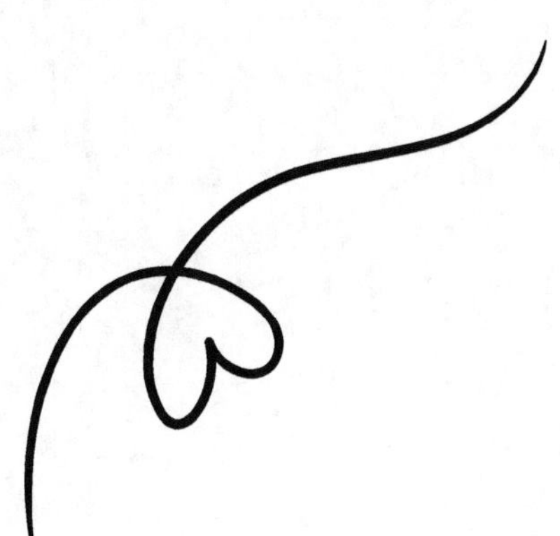

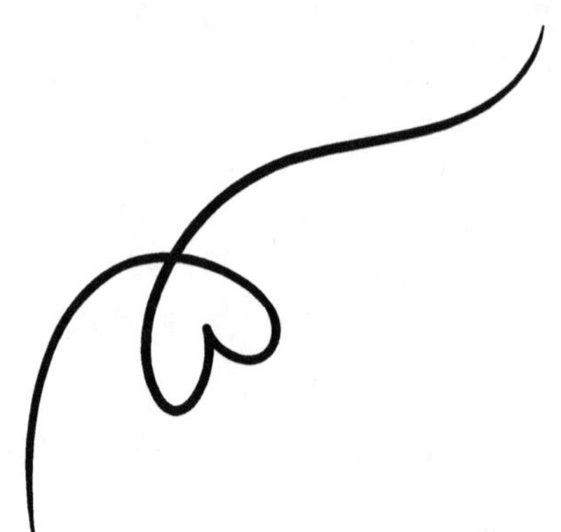

book: *dear me, love yourself*

Follow your heart
And you will find magic

Follow my Instagram page:
@moonchild.thepoet
For more magic

THANK YOU